Incredible Ironman

Contents

Written by Mary Colson

One race, three sports

In an Ironman **triathlon**, competitors swim 3.86 kilometres, cycle 180.2 kilometres and then run 42.2 kilometres. And all without a break!

Where in the world?

The first Ironman competition took place in Hawaii in 1978. Today, Ironman triathlons take place all over the world, in both hot and cold countries.

an American athlete doing an Ironman triathlon in central America, 2012

athletes finishing their swim in the Norway Ironman competition, 2012

Strength and fitness

Athletes train for many months to build up enough fitness for an Ironman competition.

Many athletes train with weights so they have strength in their arms for swimming.

Eating for energy

Before the race, **triathletes** drink lots of **liquids**. Energy drinks help them to keep going.

During the race, they eat and drink sugary food and drinks for an energy boost.

Riders drink while they're racing.

Race against the clock

The race starts at 7 a.m. and all the athletes have to finish by midnight.

The record for the fastest Ironman time is seven hours, 45 minutes and 58 seconds!

Hundreds of athletes start their swim at the same time.

Swimming kit

The swimming section is usually in mountain lakes or in the sea. Because of the cold water, triathletes sometimes wear a **wetsuit** to keep them warm.

13

Quick change!

During the race, the athletes swap their clothes and equipment in the changing area.

A fast change can give them the race lead.

Survival of the fittest

Athletes push their bodies to the limit to reach the finishing line. They have to cope with tiredness and force themselves on.

Joanna Lawn, the first woman to finish the New Zealand Ironman, in 2006

17

A race for everyone

Able-bodied and less able-bodied athletes compete together in some Ironman triathlons.

The less able-bodied athletes swim, cycle and run shorter distances. They can also have help in the changing area.

Iron Kids!

Iron Kids is a mini-triathlon for 3- to 15-year-olds. They need strength, fitness and determination, just like the adults. The Iron Kids of today might be the Ironman champions of the future.

Glossary

able-bodied   with a healthy body that has no disabilities

liquids   things like water that flow freely and are not solids or gases

triathletes   athletes who compete in a triathlon

triathlon   sports competition involving swimming, cycling and running

wetsuit   special suit that swimmers wear to keep warm

Three sports, one race

start

finish

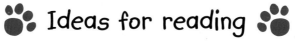 Ideas for reading

Written by Gillian Howell
Primary Literacy Consultant

Learning objectives: *(reading objectives correspond with Orange band; all other objectives correspond with Sapphire band)* read independently and with increasing fluency longer and less familiar texts; know how to tackle unfamiliar words that are not completely decodable; make notes on and use evidence from across a text to explain events or ideas

Curriculum links: P.E.

Interest words: survival, competitors, competition, Hawaii, equipment, sugary

Resources: pens, paper, drawing materials

Word count: 297

Getting started

- Read the title and discuss the cover page with the children. Ask them to speculate what an Ironman is.

- Read the blurb together. Ask the children to suggest what personal characteristics they think someone would need to be able to swim, cycle and run for hours without a break, and give reasons for their answers.

- Ask children to find the glossary and read the definitions of terms to familiarise themselves with the words before reading.

Reading and responding

- Turn to p2 and point out the term *triathlon*. Explain that *tri* means "three", and there are three sports in this competition. Ask them if they think it would be difficult to complete and whether they think they could do it.

- Listen to the children as they read, and occasionally ask them to describe any extra information they can glean from the photos. Ask them to make notes on what is needed to be successful in an Ironman triathlon as they read.